Home Life With Cats

By the same author

The *Helliconia* novels
Forgotten Life
Remembrance Day
A Tupolev Too Far

HOME LIFE WITH CATS

BRIAN ALDISS

Illustrations by KARIN VAN HEERDIN

Introduction by DESMOND MORRIS

Grafton
An Imprint of HarperCollins*Publishers*

DEDICATION

This book's Jessica's, Amy's, and Georgia's,
Because – like the cats – they're so gorgias …

Grafton
An Imprint of HarperCollins*Publishers*
77–85 Fulham Palace Road,
Hammersmith, London W6 8JB

Published by Grafton 1992
9 8 7 6 5 4 3 2 1

Text copyright © Brian Aldiss 1992
Illustrations copyright © Karin Van Heerdin 1992
Introduction copyright © Desmond Morris 1992

The Author asserts the moral right to
be identified as the author of this work

A catalogue record for this book is
available from the British Library

ISBN 0 586 21428 3

Set in Stone Serif

Printed in China

Contents

Introduction   by Desmond Morris

Of all its mysteries the one that fascinates me the most is the cat's ability to turn great writers into warm, tender slaves. Time after time, the impressive figures that thunder from the giant stage of literature can be found, in unguarded moments, crawling on hands and knees in the corners of their book-lined studies, attempting to satisfy the whim of some bouncy new kitten, or pernickety aged feline. Writing is a lonely business and there is a special bond between authors and cats, a bond that sees them sharing the long desk-hours of the day and often far into the night. An exchange of glances, a soft, stroking encounter, a brief, playful ritual, and the bond is strengthened once again. The grace of the cat and the wonderful contradiction between its utter dependence on its human owner and its aloof expressions of total independence, make it the perfect companion for the creative spirit.

And what lengths the great men have gone to! There was Edward Lear, designing his new house expressly for the comfort of his adored tabby, Foss. Sir Isaac Newton, inventing the cat-flap, to help his pets overcome that most hated of human inventions, the door. Dr Samuel Johnson, running errands for his cat Hodge 'lest the servants having that trouble should take a dislike to the poor creature'. The stories are endless – Poe, Dumas, Dickens, Capek, Eliot, they were all besotted with their feline friends, allowing themselves to unwind, to become gentle and even foolish in their company. Humanizing, therapeutic cats… .

And now another famous author comes out of the cat closet and reveals to us in a series of endearing cat poems his own long-standing love affair with these delicious, maddening animals. This is not an overnight production, lightly thrown off to satisfy a publisher and fill a slim volume. This is an assembly of 10 years of secret pennings in celebration of his adored house-pets. Never intended for publication, but eminently deserving of it, they awaken in us yet again the sheer pleasure of sharing a room with a cat, or two, or three, or… .

So, a sincere thank you to Brian for recording over the years his moments of feline fascination. I challenge anyone who has ever owned a cat not to respond instantly to these delightful poems.

Out of the Night

Out of the night that covers me,
Black as the blackest of your hats,
I thank whatever gods there be
For our innumerable cats.

It matters not how strait the gate,
How charged with punishment the scroll,
They insist on scrounging off my plate –
And I've just trodden in their bowl.

The Cats' Heaven

Maddened completely by the love of them,
I built my cats a tiny world
Complete with everything from saffron clouds
To oysters plain or deftly pearled,
Including in between those little things
That cats like best, all neatly planned:

A parrot, plumaged and loquacious, *one*;
Two bells that rang at their command;
Of poems writ in oxblood, *three*;
Four teddy bears that played some funny tricks;
Five pools of lapis lazuli,
Which each contained of dainty goldfish, *six*,
With *seven* doves about each pool
Which *ate* from leafy clumps of cyclamen;
Nine little houses built with gold;
Of catnip supermarkets more than *ten*;
And then – oh, then of mice a store
Of fubsy families at least *eleven*.
All this in ivory encased
Beneath a shell of porcelain for heaven.

'Twas done, as neat as pen or pin.
I kissed my cats and cried 'Come in'.

Although they weren't exactly scornful,
They simply sat there looking mournful...

Kittens (Two)

If one thing can make Aunt Rosie gush –
If one thing can hinder wedding
                              preparations –
If one thing can startle a grazing thrush
Or scare off wandering Alsatians –
If one thing can topple a valued eight-
Eenth century vase in quick assault –
If one thing can creep up on a tête-à-tête
And bring it to a grinding halt –

If one thing can steal a piece of raw
Meat while the cook's not looking –
If one thing can paddle in the Flor-
A, getting entangled with the cooking –
If one thing can wreck a fine weekend
By hiding somewhere out of view –
Or getting lost in the rhododend-
Rons – think what two can do!

If one thing can waste a colour film,
And instigate a vain pursuit
With camera round our blighted elm
Tree bole – then two will do it.
If one thing can ruin Uncle's visit
By weeing where it really shouldn't –
The answer's pretty clear now, is it?
Two kittens manage what one couldn't.

If one thing can ruin a brand new dress –
If one thing can chew up a vital letter –
If one thing can capture your heart,
                                    no less –
Aren't two things going to do it better?
Sotkin and Sweetpea came and saw
And conquered with their scatty jinks.
But one thing is sure – they'll soon be more
Controllable. Or so one thinks…

Slaves

O Master, O King, we depose
There are three things to which we are slave:
The belly, some stroking, a glade.
It's in hope of any of those
That we please you and always behave,
Or lie with our what-nots displayed.

We don't watch TV or read Shelley;
Just three things possess us, O King –
In hope of which you are obeyed:
A fur-lined, purr-lined belly,
An hour-long provoking stroking,
A deep jade jungle glade.

Where Have You Been?

Macramé, Macramé, where have you been?
   I climbed up the star-roof and all between.

Macramé, Macramé, what did you there?
   I cuddled up close in the paws of the Bear.

Macramé, Macramé, you tease, I've decided.
   No, master, no, master, the Bear purred like I did.

Macramé, Macramé, you must have been mad.
   Oh, master, oh, master, what times I have had!

Macramé, Macramé, you talk through your hat.
   The story's all true. Am I not your cat?

Yum-Yum

Yum-Yum is our greatest hunter.
Boney, bouncy, full of wonder,
Coat the hue of moonlit thunder,
He with cunning hunts, and love,
Till dawn comes up and moon goes under,
Watching out for one false move.

Yum-Yum is our greatest lover.
So again he's out at night,
While lady pussies purr delight.
They lie about with lambent eyes
Or scream with screams magnesium bright:
Then Yum-Yum jilts them at sunrise.

Yum-Yum is our greatest robber.
Yum-Yum is our greatest eater.
Yum-Yum's food goes down much fleeter
From his bowl than does his mother's.
So he finds that hers tastes sweeter –
Then he chases off the others.

Heatwave

In heatwaves when the waterlily floats
   With closed eye on the silent pool
   And butterflies weigh buddleia down –
   Languid peacock, meadow brown –
   Who will find a place that's cool
      For those who wear fur coats?

The wasp mob in among the fruit canes gloats
   On currants, or drinks raspberryade,
   While sprinklers on the lawns are put
   And sweating Charlotte goes barefoot –
   But who will find a cooling shade
      For those who wear fur coats?

When nettles drowse and horseflies wake,
When ponds all sink and tempers rise
   And winter's just a superstition,
When dawns are silver, moons all gold,
When clouds are shy and overs bowled –
   Our cats take up the prone position.

When old men sit with wine to chill their throats –
   Gewürztraminer, Chardonnay –
   And talk of Skye and St Nazaire
   Of rabbit pie and Robertson Hare,
   Who will find a cool place, say,
   For those who wear fur coats?

Cats' Nerves

Why do cats' nerves make the creature they serve
        Simply jump at the tiniest noise?
And why do they stare at things that aren't there
        (Which the girls do as much as the boys)?
You can't recite Keats or go out for some eats
        Without throwing them into a panic;
Should the dairyman call – any person at all,
        A neighbour, a Hoover mechanic –
They'll up from their sleep with a psychopath's leap
        To behave very niminy-pim'ny:
Such as scooting below my wife's writing bureau
        Or vanishing right up the chimney:
To emerge at nightfall expecting their rightful
        Fish dinner, or else getting stuck
In the flue by the bend. Any rescue will end
        In a shower of scratches and yuck.
Oh, what really vexes is how the reflexes
        Are madder than they can pretend;
I think I'll stop trying to NOT send them flying,
        And give them a dog for a friend …

Foxie

Fox is nimble, Fox is nice,
Fox is bad at catching Mice.
Fox is dressed in well-clipped ermine,
Fox in fact is really Birman.
Fox has seen the Southern Cross
Where the languid albatross
Sails above eternal cold.
Fox alas is growing old.
Fox can hardly see or smell you.
Oh, the tails that Fox could tell you.

Jackson

Those who make the trail to visit us,
With their snow shoes or their packs on,
Do not call on us at all:
They simply come to visit Jackson.
Oh, Jackson, with your asymmetric face,
Purr on – and yet, I can discern it, you're
A comic. When you came to us,
You spent two weeks behind the furniture.
Oh, Jackson, black-and-white, how great you'd look
In colour! Cat who never caught a mouse,
Doggone dogmatic, dearly daft –
The glory, jest, and riddle of the house.

Town-Life

When human beings first evolved,
Long after dinosaurs were dead,
They put ideas of bulk away
And went for brain instead.

And this is where the cats come in –
    On velvet paw –
    It's where the cats come in.

They spread Ideas about the world
Propelled by Thought and Sense.
The Wheel was what they dreamed up
                                first –
And then they made the Fence.

And this is where the cats come in –
    On velvet paw –
    It's where the cats come in.

As humans marched out from the woods
Or chopped and burnt them down,
The cats came bustling in their wake,
And followed them to town.

And this is where the cats come in –
    On velvet paw –
    It's where the cats come in.

The cats were kind to men. They tried
To bite or scritch-scratch them no more;
They tried to keep clean in their house –
But humans made the Door.

And this is where the cats come in –
    On velvet paw –
    It's where the cats come in.

At many awful human faults
A cat will never take offence;
Two things though they cannot stand:
The wretched Door, the horrid Fence.

And this is where the cats come in –
    On velvet paw –
    It's where the cats come in.

At first men made the cat their God,
To worship it as politic,
But all the time the work went on
Of covering the world with Brick.

And this is where the cats come in –
    On velvet paw –
    It's where the cats come in.

The bricks grew up, the fences spread,
Doors one by one were firmly closed.
The cats observing all of this
Turned off their intellects and dozed.

And this is where the cats come in –
    On velvet paw –
    It's where the cats come in.

And this is why cats sleep so much:
They wait upon that golden day
When fences, doors, and bricks are gone …
And mankind too has gone away.

And this is where the cats come in –
    On velvet paw –
    It's where the cats come in.

Then nature will come springing back,
A different culture will arise
With velvet paw and gleaming claw
And new-awakened eyes …

And this is where the cats come in –
    On velvet paw –
    It's where the cats come in.

25

Nickie

This is in memory of Nickie,
The sweetest little cat that ever stirred.
The world was better for her living.
Goldfish leapt up from puddles when she purred.
She liked to take a bath when I did,
Washing her paws with water from the tap.
She stayed awake all day, and when
Day ended she would sleep upon my lap.

Nickie and I moved out of town
(In many ways we were the perfect match);
In gratitude, she would patrol
The roof to keep the thrushes off the thatch.
She knew my car's sound and could leap
Upon it as it stopped, to press her face
Against the windscreen, welcoming.
Oh, Nickie, no cat has the heart and grace
That you had when we both were young.
And when time came for you to age and die
Who was it mourned you most of all,
Who loved you? Nickie, oh, 'twas I, 'twas I!

The Two-Kitten Problem

The problem with having two kittens
 Is, What are we going to call
Them? If one of them's going to be Peter,
 The other one has to be Paul.

The dilemma with having two kittens
 Is their names must be two of a kind:
King and Queenie, or Stalin and Hitler,
 Or even Before and Behind.

Some have naff names like Sooty and
 Fluffy,
 While Smellbags and Stinks aren't
 refined;
I don't go for Mushroom and Toadstool,
 But at least they are two of a kind.

I'd say Honeysuckle and Jasmine
 Are almost too sweet to be born.
We prefer something less sentimental,
 Like maybe Cape Wrath and Cape Horn.

Should we go then for something exotic,
 To prove that their master's a smart 'un,
And christen one Amenhotep
 And the other one Akhenaton?

(It doesn't particularly matter,
 As long as the names are quite witty,
If they're male or they're female or
 neuter –
Excepting of course to the kitty.)

So the sky is the limit. Let's twin 'em:
 We'll call them Self-Raising and Flour;
Or, to honour the neighbours, let this one
 Be Eiffel, the other be Tower.

Well, they could be Daphnis and Chloe
 To show off our erudition:
It sounds better than Mutt and Jeff does
 Or certainly Ammu and Nition.

In the next road, a family names its
 Cats after holidays. Dotty,
We call it – there's Bude, Nice and
 Sidmouth,
 And a marmalade Lanzarote.

Some American friends took a fancy
 To one fluffy new kitten and so
In honour of Kit and Joe Reed we
 Just christened it Kitten Jo.

But what could we call its brother?
 All suggestions were met with a scathing
'Oh, no' – so it wanders round nameless.
 Or answers to 'Whatsit' and 'Grey
 Thing'.

That's the problem with having two
 kittens.
 They ought to be Caesar and Cleo,
Or two of a kind. If you can't de-
Cide, try adopting a trio.

Macramé's Lament

Once in the sleepy days of Long Ago
Macramé had a bonny little son,
A ball of fluff, a dynamo of fun
(And this was Yum-Yum, though she didn't know.)

But memories are short and days have run.
She talks a lot to him, to us, to all;
And what she says in constant caterwaul
Is 'Where's my kitten?' and 'Who's seen my son?'

Travelling Cats

I had a cat that went to Mongolia:
Came back home looking much holier.

I had a cat that went to Patagonia:
Came back home looking much bonier.

I had a cat that went to Liberia:
Came back home looking superior.

I had a cat that went to Romania:
Came back home by way of Lithuania.

   I had a cat that never left Britain:
   Stayed at home and had a grey kitten.
   If it had gone to Abu Dhabi,
   Would the kitten have been a tabby?

The Cat Improvement Company

We founded the Cat Improvement Co.
For the betterment of the feline kind.
While taking their happiness to heart
We also had human good in mind.

As the blueprint shows, all those spikey
                     teeth
Were requiring removal from tiny jaws.
To improve the symmetry of the whole
We decided against the whiskers and
                     claws.

The morality, too, of the average cat
Could be definitely optimised straight
                     away
By unwinding the helix of felix's genes
And blotting out some DNA.

The result is a quadruped bound to please,
All buttery soft and cushiony nice:
It pays no attention to moths or birds,
It has an abhorrence for catching mice.

Moreover, the Cat Improvement Co.
Gives with each pet a guarantee:
'Outside bedroom windows it will not
                     yowl;
Also in corners it will not pee.'

Ceaseless research moves forward yet
As we tackle the troublesome question of
                     eyes:
What can be done to stop that glare
At spaces nothing occupies?

The CIC agenda shows
Updating is needed on silkier fur,
On gluttony, laziness, slinking,
And that aggravating purr.

The Perfect Cat is our ultimate aim
While, as far as technology reaches,
The HIC too is fulfilling its norms,
Improving the human species.

On a Favourite Goldfish

Drowned in a Bowl of Cats

Ye gods, as I sank down far beneath,
All I could see were claws and teeth,
With the glass sides pressing against their fur.
Help! Water! The world becomes a blur!

Ye gods, do you wonder I felt dismayed?
They struggled and fought and all displayed
The greediness of the feline ilk –
Five of them in a bowl of milk …

Portrait of a Cat with Lady

Luxuriously grey,
It trembles as it tells
Its love against the lady's shoulder.
Close together, they
Create a kind of spell
In the eye of the beholder.

Abstemiously fond,
She strokes it as she goes
Among her plants and seedlings growing,
Haloed in sun beyond
Her windows. In which pose
She lingers there, perhaps not knowing,

Ridiculously proud,
I watch the diverse pair:
Cat somnolent at shoulder, she
Gentle as purr is loud –
Totally unaware
Of how she charms the cat – and me.

An Evening at Home

The cats walk on our dinner tray!
As oft as he is able
Fox settles on my manuscripts,
While Yum-Yum storms the table.
Jackson is known to 'trundle' on
The wool on missus' lap.
Macramé squats upon my chest
To steal an evening nap.
We wish they'd take a wise decision
And sit and watch the television.

Tatty's Tie-Shop

(After the failure of her pie-shop,
Tatty opened up a tie-shop, 'Erewhon'. Now read on:)

Tatty the Cat took a neat little shop
(On the corner of Green Street) which only sold ties.
She stocked all the patterns from classic to pop
In more colours than show at sunrise.

Tatty opened her door with a smidgeon of qualm
For no one had wanted her pies*.
It remained to be seen if the necks of the land
Would encompass themselves with her ties.

> *[Take the head of a bloater, the lights of a sheep.
> Cover with lemonade, half an inch deep.
> Season with Christmas cake, fish skin & flour.
> Lick round the saucepan. Boil for an hour.]

But the shop was a wow from the very first day
As the customers flocked in to buy.
Though some merely wanted to stop for a chat,
The majority needed that tie.

And who were these customers? Well, most were men
But I mustn't deceive you thereby,
For many a woman slipped into the shop
And secretly purchased a tie.

And not only humans! One day about six,
An elegant Keeshond stopped by,
Addressed Tatty Cat in the suavest of tones
And bought a maroon-and-puce tie.

He was swaggering off when a Poodle appeared.
The colours attracted its eye,
And before you could say 'Mack the Knife' it ran in
And demanded a similar tie.

The fashion was started. Soon humans and dogs
Were queueing to give it a try.
But narry a cat came inside Tatty's shop
To deck itself out in a tie.

She could sell any puppy a tie with bone pattern
Any upper class lady a tie of white satin,
A cravat with guitars on to anyone Latin,
A tall guy, a Great Dane – a tie that was long,
An undertaker – a tie with a hearse on:
But MOGGIES? Forget it. They knew it was wrong.
Which just goes to prove what I've said all along –
You can't tie up a cat like a dog or a person …

Snacks

The English language has a little word
Which cats (who know no English) find absurd:
In fact, it makes them roll upon their backs.
   It's 'Snacks'.

Sweetpea particularly has the power
To summon us at some impromptu hour
With awful cries, to tell us what he lacks.
   It's snacks.

It's snacks – a little bit of this or that,
Some old spaghetti or the gammon fat
They need at 3 a.m. … To fill the cracks
   It's snacks.

I too fall victim to this awful yen –
Mars Bars at tea break, slice of cake at ten –
If there's one habit that I ought to axe
   It's snacks.

Who Owns the House?

Our family house has seven bedrooms in it,
Some old armchairs, a tablecloth, a linnet,
A picture of a storm at sea, some clocks,
A large old fridge, some stairs, a music box.
What most distinguishes our home, we think,
Is not the fire-irons or the kitchen sink,
But Jackson, Black Thing, Yum-Yum Boy, and Fox.

And here at once I must apologise,
For 'Black Thing's' not a name but a disguise.
All of our cats have several names. Fox knows he
Can be addressed as Smoke or Posey;
Jackson responds (or not) to Peter Gordon,
His secret name to save him being bored. On
Sundays, 'Grey Thing' christens Yum-Yum's nosey.

It's these four cats who own, all unawares,
Linnet (in cage!), the tablecloth, the chairs,
The painting of the storm, the various clocks,
The stairs, the fridge, the music box that locks,
The kitchen sink, the irons, the seven beds.
They all exist for those four sleepy heads –
Jackson, Macramé, Yum-Yum Boy, and Fox.

Riddle

My first is in Kitten but not in Eye
My second in Apple but not in Pie
My third is in Rabbit but not in Rat
My fourth is in Bristle but not in Cat
My last is in the question Why?

My whole is like a mixed-up dye.
       What am I?

How I Swam Out to Sea with My Cat

How I Swam Out to Sea with My Cat …
As the notion swam into my mind
I thought, 'Well, a title like that
Simply must tow a poem behind.'

Daring Jackson and I are alone on the languorous length of a beach
On an October coast without coastguards or signs of the least habitation.
He gives me the kind of a look that would easily ripen a peach
And human and cat we go plunging head first in that great inundation.

It's chill in the water but once through the breakers we slightly relax.
Since the dog-paddle clearly is barred we decide on the butterfly crawl,
At which Jackson excels. Or sometimes we essay a few strokes on our backs,
As we head for the deeps in response to an urgent adventurous call.

We swam out a mile. There we had to call truce, for a premature star
Burned aloft, while through billowing sea mist the sunset resembled a ghost shrine.
We floated and listened. The swell now was still. And because of the haar
Neither I nor the cat – who climbed on to my cranium – sighted the coastline.

Bedraggled was Jackson, and I little better. Adrift in the haze,
We could be considered extremely foolhardy, sufficient to miff any
Friends who might see us. So be it. Yet Jackson – his eyes were ablaze
With pure joyance, as if in the grip of a super-mammalian epiphany!

A spirit moved over the unsleeping brine-wastes; we both felt the thrill
Of supreme revelation. Adroitly, the cat took command of our union.
By a gesture he showed he had mastered the power of speech and would fill
Me with wisdom unguessed. Then he spoke in a low voice of mystic communion –

But my Muse simply let me down flat,
And what Jackson said we sha'n't know.
How I Swam Out to Sea with My Cat
Was a title sans poem in tow.

A Lion for Tea

I was cutting back the laurels in our drive –
On Monday, this was, some time after three –
And so I didn't see the lion arrive
Alive
And all spruced up to join our cats for tea.

My wife was over at the Garden Centre,
And so the cats were left to do their best
As hosts. After discussion, Sotkin lent a
Magenta
Dish with bread and fish on to their guest.

They followed this with cream served in a bowl.
The grateful lion, impressed by feline morals,
Tucked each cat in his mane and took a droll
Stroll
Round the garden. (I hid in the laurels.)

The Cat in the Cathedral *or* Rat Apocalypse

While the choir chants evensong,
Prowling through the sounding cloister
Goes the cat – a furred Jehovah,
God of Wrath, to mice who throng
In organ pipes, or elsewhere roister
When the Sabbath Day is over.

    Stained glass saints, as in a wager,
    Pose with Grace at fingertips –
    Quite forgetting cats must stage a
      Rat Apocalypse.

While hymns tell of human striving
For forgiveness, absolution,
Lo, the cat breeds endless kitties:
Heaven's against not Sin but thriving
Rodenthood. It's Retribution
Till the final Nunc Dimittis.

    Stone apostles, minor, major,
    Taste God's Word upon their lips –
    Quite forgetting cats must stage a
      Rat Apocalypse.

While the human congregation,
For Salvation à la psalter
Kneels, some lesser denizens
Undergo wild consternation:
Parish cat behind the altar
Dishes out some last Amens.

    Haloed angels, sweeter, sager,
    Guide the Blest on Heavenward trips –
    Quite forgetting cats must stage a
      Rat Apocalypse.

The day Thou gavest, Lord, is ending –
And, alas, in some confusion:
Nature's red in teeth and toes.
Though the sermon's for extending
Peace on Earth, it's an illusion
Till the cat has killed its foes.

    Twelve disciples all presage a
    Time when Joy knows no eclipse –
    Quite forgetting cats must stage a
      Rat Apocalypse.

The Poor Man's Cat

My master he stroked me before marching out to the fight
    Poor man.
His brow was all furrowed, his lips were unusually tight
    Poor man.
He left me some ox cream and as he went out of the room
He blew me a farewell which mingled affection with gloom.
Now I knew he was brave and was famed for his tactical flair
So I skipped to the window to see how my master would fare
    Poor man.
All the army was armoured but master with only a shield
Strode forth like a lion to see what the foeman would yield.
From their ranks came a boy with a sling, under-sized, yellow-haired
Who had at my master before he was really prepared
    Poor man.
And the stone from the sling caught my master a blow on his brow
So wounding he fell to the ground. With a fearful *miaou*
I ran out – but before he could rise or consort with the dead
The boy with the sling shot had cut off my poor master's head
    Poor man.
Those days had been good – now I'm merely a wraith among men
For no one can stroke me as Master Goliath did then
    Poor man
    Poor master and man.

Mutual Regard

The elderly man looks down at the cat
And the cat looks up at the elderly man.
'Well, what in the world do you make of that?',
Each thought as they stared.
                                    By some heavenly plan
It happened that God sat down for a span
And left Creation to boil in the pan
And said, as he watched them, 'Well, just fancy that –
The pussy cat sits and looks up at the man
And the man looks down at the cat.
And since I'm the Author of Riddles, my hat! –
I SHOULD understand it, if anyone can,
Why the elderly man looks down at the cat
And the cat looks up at the man ...'

First Birthday

I'm writing this poem for Karin
(I'm the only cat who can write)
To thank her for all of the presents:
A hair brush, a big bakelite
Mug, some catnip, a gold paper crown.
(I look sweet in it.) Then till we burst
We ate rat pie (the finest in town)
And mice Karin baked for my birthday (my first).

I invited my two closest friends,
That humorous leopard Hortense
(She lives round the corner) and Ivy,
Whose purr doesn't make any sense
(And she's bigger than I am). The party
Was fun. We played games and were able
To savour the cake (herring flavour).
(Thanks, Karin, for painting us all at the table.)

Rules

I'm not allowed out till I'm bigger.
I've got to consider my figure.
My missus has only got three cups,
So I mustn't play games with the teacups.
I may not do a mess in the basket
Or flowerpot. 'Ginger' – don't ask it
Indoors, 'cos it's only a stray.
Don't sleep on the cushion all day,
Don't flop on the flower shelf at night.
With my brothers and sisters don't fight.
Don't scratch when they're tying your bow on.

And so on and so on and so on …

All these rules cause the brain of a kitten to fog.
When I grow up I'm determined I shall turn into a large ferocious black dog.

Relating to the Pet

    Researchers in California
With the aid of much tax-payers' dough
Have made the world's best breakthrough ever.
Though it's new, though it's novel, I know
It's also a bit of old folklore
That granny said never forget:
    It's good to relate to your pet.

Keep stroking your kitten –
Five minutes a day
Involvement with persian or tabby
Will soothe your cholesterol away.

Keep fondling the ferret
Also your aardvark.
It does more for your circulation
Than yoga or jogs round the park.

Keep grooming the goldfish
Keep tickling the toad.
Just remit it for one day –
That could be the end of the road.

    Yes, it's good to relate to your gerbil
    As science has recently proved.
    There's a low tactile plus to stick insects,
    But, god, how they need to be loved!

You must always chat up your canary
And polish your parrot. They may
At times seem a bit airy-fairy
Or lacking in smart things to say,
But they're ace on the aorta.
Your life can be longer not shorter
Now that science delivers the truth,
For those wizards in California
Have hit on the secret of youth:
So, folks, I am happy to warn ya
You don't have to keep taking the tablets
Or spending your Sundays in bed.
Relax, throw your crutches away now
And dandle the dormouse instead.
So keep hugging your hedgehog,
Keep embracing the budgie:
They're going to increase your survival
Whenever the lymph glands get sludgey.

Keep rubbing the rottweiler,
Pray that you don't get bitten.
The way to avoid a stroke is –
   Keep stroking the kitten ...

The Cat Speaks

Sunlight that lingers, fleeting and pure,
Eternally changing, insecure:
I'm that. While your parvenue
Dog is your servant, obsequious and odd –
I'm elemental, elusive as god.
   I don't think like you.

By a whisker I'm grateful for comforts received;
I'm a glutton for sleeping, but never deceived
By your sycophant words.
For cats must survive in the cruel world of man
Where more lives are despatched than ever I can
   In my way with the birds.

Michael, the Cycling Cat

On my racing bi-cycle
I cycle with Michael
'Cos Michael's a cycling cat.

In sly ways we try ways
Through highways and byways
'Cos Michael's a cycling cat.

We used to read Proust too,
Whose mots justes seduced you,
But Michael's a cycling cat.

With pedals ablaze –
There goes Walton-on-Naze,
And wasn't that Bas-
ingstoke in the haze?
But this boy is no cloister-
ed cat, World is his oyster
That opens up just like a gate …
The horizon is Michael's
home straight.
I've found that I'm bound
To go round foreign ground
After Michael, the cycling cat.

If you wheeze, 'Where to,
please?', he
Says, 'Easy – Tblisi!'
'Cos Michael's a cycling cat.

This cat'll
Rattle through Battle,
Muscat or Seattle.
At Medicine Hat'll
Scoot on in fine fettle:
He's in Cap Ferat or
He's through Ulan Bator
And next Boca Raton –
There's Stretton and Stratton!
With no cap or hat on
He hurtles through Hatton
To be briefly seen
By the shores of Katrine
And the Kattegat too.
In far Kathmandu
He has been …
   So – Scat! –
It's been incred-
ible, King of the Pedals is
earning his med-
als like that!
Make way for this cheetah,
Kilometre-eater,
World-beater –
None fleeter
Than Michael the cycling
   Cycling cyclone
The cycling
   cyclonic
      cat!

The Lost Grave

This is the place – no, it's here – wait, it's there –
But I know that I planted a moon-shaped stone –
Well it's somewhere quite near to this old gnarled yew –
That Baby Cat lies in the earth all alone.

She was Baby Cat always – adopted when young
Quite wild from the Animal Sanct'ry. It showed
When she wouldn't be nursed. Yet we loved her – and lost
Her the day she decided to go on the road.

So we buried her then – it was autumn, I think –
Somewhere here – and our tears were all silently shed.
Leaves blew and snow came – but it's five years ago.
It was somewhere near here. Baby Cat, are you dead?

I see you so clear in your woolly black socks,
With your smart tawny coat and your purr deep and slow,
And the litter you bore us in Tim's bottom drawer.
I see you so clear – but it's five years ago…

Now is a week since Christmas, and the year
Postscripts in pallor. Ice freckles the pond,
Frost waits in hedges. At its most austere
The season bids us think what lies beyond
Our daily life. We burn the Yuletide log,
Hoping to revive the withered sun
Whose ghost glints through the holly trees. In fog
We walk with thoughts of those whose day was done
Long days ago: whose bones as they dissolve
Are cryptograms for memories to solve.

64